L
A Colle

Written by Artemis L. Tally

Disclaimer – These are my memories, from my perspective, and I have tried to represent events as faithfully as possible. I have changed people's names in order to protect individual's privacy.

Copyright © 2021 Artemis L. Tally

All rights reserved.

Paperback ISBN: 9798726904368

First Paperback edition: March 2021

Cover Art by Finn Marcks
Cover Art formatted by Esperanza Garay-Negrón

Printed by Amazon/Amazon Direct Publishing
Independently Published

Table of Contents

Small Note from the Author ... 6

Chapter 1 – First of Many
When Love Reaches Its Limits ... 8
My First Suitor ... 10
My First Flight ... 11
Twisted Tragedy ... 12
Change of Season ... 14
Digital Romance ... 15
Love Letter to My First Love ... 16
The Arrival ... 17
Disconnect ... 18
A Familiar Setting ... 19

Chapter 2 – Dangerous World
Dance with the Devil ... 22
Defiled Temple ... 24
A New Hope ... 25
The Great Divide ... 26
The Wolf and I ... 27
Reconstruction ... 28

Chapter 3 – Smoke and Mirrors
Empty Gestures in Empty Bedrooms ... 30
In the Dark ... 31
Secret Thoughts Addressed to a Crush ... 32
Halloween Party ... 33
Off to the Races ... 34
His Next Trick: A Disappearing Act ... 36
Truth Comes to the Light ... 38
In the Dark - Part 2 ... 40
Fighting Off the Gray ... 42
In the Dark - Part 3 ... 44
A Hope Meditation ... 45

Chapter 4 – Finding Balance

Change of Season - Part 2	47
Desire	48
Living in Color	49
Polyamory	50
Eclipse	51
The Final Straw	53
When Love Reaches Its Limits - Part 2	54
Goodbye Love	55
A Game of Desire	56
Empty Gestures in Empty Bedrooms – Part 2	57
Cotton Candy	58
Aiming for a Better Version	59

Chapter 5 – A New Dawn

Love Redefined	61
Ode to the Strongest Woman I Know, My Mother	63
Love Letter for CD	65
Love Letter for JD	66
Love Letter for DH	67
Love Letter for EE	68
Love Letter for FM	69
Love Letter to AS & CS	70
Love Letter to E&K	71
Kindness Within	72
What Love Actually Is	74

Small Note from the Author

I never had a guide on how to live my life. Gay and transgender folks don't fit into the mold society has created. The American Dream doesn't work for Black Queer and Trans people. We can't live in that image because we were never in mind when it was created. Homophobia, racism, transphobia and many other oppressions intersect and form a barrier that no one can cross without getting torn apart.

I had to venture out on my own path and that led me to some really dangerous places. Men, much older than me, would come in and try to use me. It took me a long time to realize what was happening. Then I had to learn how to love and I will admit that I didn't always know how to do that. So many lessons came from my experiences and it shaped me into the person I am today.

A variety of different topics will be discussed in this poetry book. I want to let the reader know that some serious and heavy topics will be touched upon in this story. Love, sex, betrayal, break ups, hard nights, loneliness, sadness, negative views of self, and sexual assault are all addressed in my debut book.

I want to give a proper content warning now and before the poems featuring talk of sexual assault. I think these poems are important to be kept in. They are a part of my story and I don't want to hide them away in a closet. They need to be addressed and taken seriously.

Some of these poems were written during the time and others are a reflection of events that happened. I put my emotions into this project and it has helped me close some chapters in my life.

I hope readers can relate to some things.
I hope I can show the world in a new light.
I hope that this can bring someone hope for a better tomorrow.

I hope this teaches someone else how to fly. No one should be stuck on the ground forever. There are so many realms of possibilities we should all aim to see. That's how we can change the world. We dream it and move toward the horizon.

Chapter 1
First of Many

When Love Reaches Its Limits
Love is like a scrapbook
Full of beautiful memories and moments.
You open the snapshots in your mind
A sudden burst explodes inside your chest

For a moment, the air is lighter
A technicolor panorama appears before your eyes
We yearn for this moment to last forever

We never dream that this feeling would ever end,
How could we ever try to be rid of something
So precious?

Something so close to perfect,
Even the gods would envy us, simple mortals.

But what happens when the love fades
and snuffs out the flame?

Love has a sharp, bitter sting when you must
release someone you've known so long.
The twisted feeling in your gut when you lose
what you hold dearest is nearly unbearable

Every force in life must face a death eventually
Every lost maintains a harmony
Love is many things,
but it isn't free from nature's wrath

So why do we choose to love anyway?
I suppose one could ask the same about why we live..

To both of these questions,
I have a thought that comforts me

Even when love can't go on,
Just remember the good that came before

Cherish those moments dearly

Hold them in your heart and
Pray to the Heavens that they never fade.

We can't recreate the past,
But we can aim for a better version

My First Suitor
An unfortunate first appeared in my life at 15.
A boy showed interest in me
We were both boys,
but he was older than me

I had just come out
to my best friend a week before
She turned his gaze to me
I couldn't help the fact that I enjoyed the attention

My first boyfriend,
My first broken promise,
My first disappointment.

He was the first boy I allowed myself to date
He was the first to ever stand me up
(and he had the audacity to do it twice!)
I stood foolishness in that lobby,
waiting for any sign of the boy that I liked

It hurt like hell when the realization sank in
He wasn't coming.
But it taught me a valuable lesson
I don't deserve to be humiliated like that by any man

No one will ever make me feel like that EVER again

I can do better than that

My First Flight
He opened a door I never knew existed
I crept out of my cage
Careful and cautious
Expecting something to drop,
To place me back into my box,
But it didn't happen.

I spread my wings
Prepare for take off.
It was time to soar into the unknown.
I was lifted, higher and higher.
I flapped helplessly
But soon, there wasn't enough wind for me

Helplessness gripped me like a python.
I quickly descended out of orbit
The cold earth rumbled upon impact.
Dust and confusion crowded around me
I couldn't cry now,
Everyone was watching me

But I finally made a decision
I wasn't going back into my box.
I had fallen in love with the sky
And all the possibilities that it held
How could I ever say no to that majestic beauty?

I just had to wait for my chance
The wind will pick up one day
I will fly higher than I could ever imagine
I just had to wait for it...

Twisted Tragedy
My second boyfriend appeared a month later
He was sweet and shy and funny
I thought, *this was a nice change
from the jerk who left me with no warning*
The flirting and time spent together felt nice
At least at first.

Soon, in the cover of night,
He revealed his twisted game
He tied a rope around my neck
The noose tightened against my skin
Time slowed, along with my airflow
I gasped and scrambled for freedom

He pulled me closer and promised to never let me go.
I didn't want him to stay,
Fear had overwhelmed me
I had forgotten all about the good.

I was held hostage for a solid month
He needed help, but I couldn't be the hero he craved
I couldn't even save myself,
How could I be expected to be his Superman?
My body wasn't made of steel,
Only blood and flesh and fear like him

I had reached my first point of no return
If I leave, he said he'll kill himself.
Death, complete and irreversible.
No matter how hard I would scrub,
His blood will stain my hands crimson for all eternity
That's the vow he made without my consent
The curse he placed upon my conscious

My heart was heavy and conflicted
I didn't see the manipulation forming at the time
All I saw was a boy who needed someone to save him
I wasn't that man for him, but he was convinced otherwise

We were never destined to have a glorious 'happily ever after'
We were stuck performing a tragedy worthy of a Shakespearian play.

The knife was between us on the table
Who would be the first to grab it and seal the ending of the other?

This can't be it for me,
I thought as my heart thumped like a drum
I just discovered this world,
how could it close so quickly?
What am I doing here?

He can't just force me to love him
I had barely known him for two months
We weren't destined to be wed
We were high school students!
Young and immature
We haven't experienced a **portion** of what life has to offer
This can't be my end

I grab the knife and throw it to the floor
I won't be a romantic hostage.
I have my own wants and desires
They should be respected and acknowledge

A couple is made of two people,
Not just the fantasy of one depressed child.

The lights fade to black,
I stand and walk to the exit
The Final Act comes to a close as the curtain falls.
A definite conclusion to a story of love and manipulation.
I close the door behind me without looking back

"Goodbye"

Change of Season
Butterflies flutter along the spring breeze
A new feeling emerges after a long winter
There is a shift in the atmosphere

The sky was rough and the winds were as sharp as a knife
Now the sky is pink and the wind is only a whisper

Things are better
A new reign is coming into the kingdom
I am finally happy.

This is closer to what I saw on the big silver screen
A love was in bloom and flourishing before my very eyes
I was the main protagonist in this feature
And I couldn't be more happy to finally experience what I always saw
Love.
Such an elusive sensation...

The earth is blooming and growing with each moment
The darkness was finally over.
The sun rise was the most beautiful sight

Maybe this will be the start of the happy ending everyone had promised me

Digital Romance
A notification vibrates on my phone
My heart leaps high into the sky
I know who it is
I've been waiting for this all day

I hop over to my laptop and sign in
The laptop roars to life
and rumbles into the normal routine.
I open Skype and wait
My heart beats harder and harder with each second.
When will he call?

The ding of a notification makes me jump with joy
The call bubble appears in the middle of my screen

Answer : Decline

Answer
I smile and exhale a sigh of relief and comfort

I am home once more.

Love Letter to my First Love
Dear Ben,

You have always loved me to the best of your ability
Even though we are separated by thousands of miles,
You always supported me
Better than anyone I had known in person at the time
Validated me in all that I chose to pursue
You never stopped believing in me and that meant the world to me
You always cared and looked out for me
I could always count on you to make me smile when I needed it most

We always made time for one another
Even with thousands of miles and several hours between us,
We always made it a point to watch shows and movies,
Caught up on YouTube videos together.
You never felt too far away…

Despite being the farthest person away from me,
You always made me feel as if I could call at any point
Ready to catch me when I fell.
Ready to pick up the pieces when life crumbled
To share a life forever together,
And everything would be okay…

You showed me what love should be like
You showed me what real kindness was
You showed me what it meant to truly love myself
You were the first light to shine so bright
When I was in the sea of darkness.
My boat was set adrift long before you appeared
All hope was far gone by this point

You brought me back from the brink of death and destruction
You cared for me as I traveled the valley of dread alone.
You showed me what it was to live again
I can never thank you enough for what you gave me.
Love, Artemis

The Arrival
Waiting at the terminal's entrance
My heart was playing Mario Kart
My stomach felt like it is in my throat
My thoughts jumbled into a huge mess

It's too late to go back now.
He's flown from another continent to be at my side
He traveled across the world,
Just to see me
That held a meaning much bigger than I had imagined

I see a familiar shape in the distance with adequate luggage.
I know his frame anywhere and my heart skips a beat
Our eyes meet and my heart stops for a moment

My Love,
Alive and in the flesh.

No more hiding behind a computer screen.
No more 0's and 1's making combinations
No screen to bridge the gap between us

We hug each other for the first time.
We kiss and feel my lips join yours.
This feels so joyous and wonderful.

And everything else goes away
Everything else goes away,
And it's only us in the world.

Disconnect
He held me with a gentleness I've never experienced before
Softer than a fresh flower pedal on a spring afternoon
The kindest boy I have ever met
And he was sweeter than honey
His thoughtfulness matched my own, and that meant a lot.
But something didn't connect
Like a wire that short-circuits
Like a burnt-out conductor
The transmission is lost somewhere along the line
And I have no idea how to fix the problem

What is happening to me?
My life was slow and steady and predictable,
And that all changed when I left home for college
Time flew by me and I didn't even notice for quite some time

Long afternoon talks every day transformed into once a week
I met so many people and attended so many events...
I was swept up by the new, shiny reality I was witnessing
My phone fell to the wayside along with his messages
I don't notice how far I wandered until it was too late
The miles between us finally felt real
The vastness of the entire ocean between us scared me
The time difference found a new level that intimidated me

I didn't know my beginning would be our end
Never once did I intend to let you down
But once the landslide began,
There was no escaping its grip.

The glass was shattered between us
Our tether cut too short
There was no way your warmth could reach me now
We were continents away from one another after all

I never meant for this to happen
You will always have a piece of my heart and that's okay with me
I hope you cherished our time as much as I do...

A Familiar Setting
I sit alone once again
Loneliness is my only companion at the moment
But I'm not upset.
I'm at peace.

It's time for someone new to settle in beside me
A new lover that will satisfy my needs
Someone that can stop my heart from craving such wild fantasies

I place my heart on a Grindr profile for all to see
I will find someone to hold me with every inch of their being
Their light will finally drive away the darkness that lingers in my head

But will I ever be satisfied?
Truly content with life
That's such a big order to complete

Can a single man ever accomplish the task of loving me again?
Gods, I hope so

I dream of someone driving away all the pain I've acquired
but something tells me that isn't in the cards for me

Maybe I will be forever alone and loneliness will reign

Maybe this future lover isn't the proper answer I need,
But it sure is the answer I desire.

Peace, that's what I desire the most

Chapter 2
Dangerous World

Quick Author's Note
Content Warning – Sexual Assault

I wanted to put a content warning before you continue to the next poem. I talk about the time I was raped in "Dance with the Devil" and "Defiled Temple".

Both of these poems are raw and emotional and a bit graphic (especially Dance with the Devil). I think these two poems are important and I understand that they are very heavy. They are a part of my story and I wouldn't be telling the whole truth without including them.

The action of one man stayed with me for a long time afterwards. I've talked with professionals and have healed a great deal since that event. It took a long time, but I took back the agency that was stolen from me.

If you or anyone you know has been sexually assaulted, I want to say that I'm sorry that happened and it's not your fault. You didn't do anything to deserve that.

There are great resources out there that you could reach out to. It's a heavy burden and no one should go through it. Here is the number for the National Sexual Assault Hotline for those living in the United States (800.656.4673). They can listen to your needs and give you resources that are close to your region.

It's not a perfect system and there may be gaps as wide as the Grand Canyon, but I hope you can take the steps you need in order to heal and move forward.

I wish for all those reading this to find safety and hope and peace in their life, today and every day. You are special and important and I hope you never forget that.

Much love,
A.L.T

Dance with the Devil

A variety of suitors approach me.
Newly 18 and the world was my oyster
Baby-faced and innocent,
I walked into the lion's den.
I thought I knew what I was doing,
But life isn't as simple as the movies shown

Sure I ran into knights in shining armor.
They were complete gentlemen
Opened my door,
Pulled out my chair,
Paid for my dinner after lovely conversations,
The whole nine yards.

These men would sweep me off my feet,
But what goes Up must come back Down.

One man saw me falling and made a wish upon my body
The vile creature craved sexual satisfaction
A fantasy fulfilled without my permission
Feasting on my warm body
Stealing my blood, my soul, my flesh

Ravaged and violated
Rough hands tore my skin
He entered me as I protested
My voice echoed back to me,
So I know my words aren't silent,
But he never got the message.

He just shushed me and whispered lies into my ears
My wants and boundaries tossed aside like an old toy
This was a simple act of domination to him

A two player game of trust and intimacy
Perverted into a new single player game
He had the only controller
A fast track to a perfect KO victory

I never stood a chance

After a while, Hope packed up and left me to the wolves
Light had left the world and Darkness never felt so vast
A numbness overcame me and soiled everything around me
My skin wasn't mine anymore and I didn't want anything to do with it

I lay still,
I lay unhappy,
I lay waiting for the end...

How did I get here?

Powerless and spiraling
No one could ever prepare me for the impact of this one action...

There was so much promise,
So much hope for pleasure,
And it was snatched out of my hands.
The only feeling that remained was disappointment and pain

I thought I could handle the task,
I thought hooking up with strangers was easy
I didn't know the Devil had invited me into his home
His smile was too pretty and I didn't see the signs
I paid dearly for that mistake

After that night, Sex would never be the same for me
Relationships were tarnished before they even started
A hard exterior stationed itself around my heart

It would take years to undo the damage from one single night,
I didn't know how long it would take to process that trauma
All I knew in the moment was that I felt disgusting and incomplete...

Defiled Temple

The greedy and trifling merchants invaded my temple
They placed their wares and shops on top of my altars,
They rearranged the pews and made room for their business

Nothing is sacred to these beasts who roam the earth
They only care for their own gain and entertainment
They always throw me aside when they climax.
I'm only a placeholder for them and their seed

As the sun sets across the land,
They pack everything they had brought
And left just as quickly as they came.

Inside I was alone and felt as cold as winter
My mental strength depleted
All of my resources exploited
My body was in ruins

I was sore and broken and blood covered the walls
I never imagined anyone could do this much damage
Tears swelled in me and I finally collapsed

My own arms wrapped around my vessel,
I couldn't trust a man to do this but I needed the safety of touch
There was power exchanged when two people embrace one another
It didn't work so well with only one pair of arms, but I tried nonetheless

For months, no matter what I tried, I always felt cold.
I laid on that barren floor for many seasons
How could I ever be at peace in my own home after this destruction?

A New Hope
Some time passed
I found an oasis hidden in my desert of mistrust
I met Gay and Trans people who were like me

We formed a community,
We called one another family,
We stood with one another.

We stationed ourselves in a beautiful Castle.
It overlooked a majestic lake
Located in the heart of the Kingdom
A perfect location for a perfect stand-in family

I was finally blooming once again after my long winter
I had a family that actually understood my struggle
Or so I thought…

Life had to remind us how fragile our alliance truly was
We got too comfortable in a house of cards

It only took one match
To set everything ablaze
The structure came tumbling down

When the smoke cleared,
The Castle and its inhabitants would never be the same again

The Great Divide
I spent 3 long months back in my hometown
It was a hard time for me
All I had known before felt different,
In reality, nothing had changed

But maybe I was the one who changed.
The picture I once held was ripped to shreds
And I had no idea how to place it back together
I felt like a foreigner in my own hometown

I yearned for my stand-in family
I had missed the Castle, my pseudo-home.
A place of fantasy to hide from reality

I returned to the West side of Michigan
As I approached, I saw a ghastly sight
My Castle was in shambles

The ones I called family were at one another's throat
Factions had spawned and a war was raging
My paradise was in disrepair
Flames stretched to the skies and casted my world into darkness
I cried so hard and feared what would come next

That's when He stalked in
A Wolf appeared in the tall grass
He saw me with lustful eyes and imagined all sorts of dark fantasies
I saw him as an escape from my crumbling social support system
We both pursued each other, hiding our true motives from one another

The pact was made after a few weeks: Boyfriends

The Wolf and I
Things were easy at first.
The Wolf was a good distraction
An escape with a getaway car included in the package
We would have nice talks on our travels
He wasn't exactly what I needed,
But he fit the bill well enough

There were many warning signs on this highway,
But me, being the passenger,
I decided to compromise
I'd let the driver handle things.
A fire ignited in the backseat.
I ignored it and kept my eyes forward

This is my way out.
Danger lurked in the background.
My days were numbered,
But I still kept my eyes forward.

Sweat collected on my neck
The fire started to burn my skin
I grit my teeth and grinned
I had to make this work
In my eyes, this was the sacrifice of love

"I can make this work",
I told myself this over and over and tried to believe it too
That was until I became the sacrifice
Stripped and thrown away for an idol
An idol, that mimicked my body,
But that silent cow was easier prey for the Wolf
My pact with The Wolf was officially terminated,
Shredded and thrown to the side
I watched the burning car ride off into the sunset

I wanted to cry,
But I wouldn't let that damned wolf get anything else from me.

Reconstruction
It was time for me to step outside,
Into the real world once again
I had to face the flames of the Castle eventually,

Luckily, I wasn't alone for this venture
I discovered a new family that was truly loyal and loving and kind
A diverse variety of shades and backgrounds
All bound by love and trust

Our love wasn't superficial anymore
This love dug itself deeper, like a tree's roots
Tunneling into the dirt to form a proper foundation
Wrapped around all of us and provided shelter during the storm
Provided nutrients through the hard winters
Our tree stretched out much farther than we ever could have imagined

They held my hand as we surveyed the smoldering damage
Our home may have been shattered,
But we could pick up the pieces
Merge them all into something stronger than before
A gift that we could pass on for generations after us

We held the new keys of the Castle in our hands
It was our duty to construct a masterpiece
A safe stop to give peace and solace to any queer traveling alone
A place where they could rest after their long journey
Help them grow into who they are destined to be.
A home that would allow them to build their own family

We could move forward,
With the help of one another.
We could prevail,
But there was a lot of work that had to be done first
Good thing I could trust this new faction of mine.
I found a true family

Chapter 3
Smoke and Mirrors

Empty Gestures in Empty Bedrooms
A string of flings began for the summer
I would go through bedrooms like they were storefronts in a mall
A night full of sex and empty gestures would pass in an instance
Then I would wake in their arms
Their grasp felt like I was being held by hollow specters.
Cold and empty like the wind in winter

I would gather my belongings
and escape into the dew filled dawn
Most didn't pay me any attention
My purpose was already completed
They had already busted their nut
Their slumber and satisfaction made me jealous
I wish I could sleep as easy as they could.
How do you sleep soundly next to a stranger?

It didn't matter.
Onto the next man to repeat the process
A lustful night
An act of flesh satisfaction
A cuddle session, if I was lucky enough,
Then I would slip out into the night,
Just before dawn
The constellations watched from above
I wonder if they could spot my tears from that high?

I remember a question someone asked me once,
Will you ever be satisfied?
I didn't know how to answer that question at first...
I'm starting to figure out though...

In the Dark
Waiting for something
Waiting for anything
The pain of loneliness grips my entire being.

It's been a hard day.
I begin to feel ugly
I begin to think no one will settle for me

Maybe the idea of me attracts people
But I never seem to be able to seal the deal,
Always one step behind.
Always the last to know

No one thinks about my feelings
They all use me for my listening ear,
But no one can listen to me.
Or maybe they can
and I simply never gave them a chance

Why can't I ever be satisfied?

Why can't I ever be the first choice?

The only choice...

Secret Thoughts: Addressed to a Crush
Do you ever wonder about me?
Do you ever look to my body and yearn for a closer look
A deeper touch?

Do you ever feel the connection we have?
Sometimes it's so tangible
It's like a string between us
The link that binds us both

I know you don't choose me
You have never chosen me
I'm not even on your list, right?
Just tell me the truth so I can be free.

Do you think of me when you are about to sleep?
Do you wonder about me as I undress?
Why can't I just know the truth?
Put an end to the whole affair…
Confirm my suspicion or just tell me I'm crazy

Why do you try to keep me close?
Why do you always keep me in mind?
Please give me the answer I hope for.
The happy ending I dream of,
But can never seem to manifest into reality.

Am I ready for love?
Or just desperate enough to settle for someone
Who won't leave me behind in the dark?

Halloween Party
It is time to set the stage for a new suitor
After many days and many weeks and many moons
And many different dates that didn't lead to anything significant
It was Halloween and I was excited to go out and mingle

I arrived to a house party with my friends
We all came through looking great in our costumes
Even though Michigan in late October is chillier than most places,
I made a point to show as much skin as possible.

Alcohol flowed endlessly into plastic cups
Weed smoke wafted through the air
Music beats bumped as people danced in tandem

My eyes meet the gaze of an attractive man
The attraction is clearly mutual as he crossed the room to greet me
He compliments my costume and I return the gesture

He introduces himself, Jacob
I introduce myself and make a note to remember his name
My mind wanders south as we continue to flirt with one another
Desire clearly hung in the air

My friends gathered and prepared to leave
I told this new suitor farewell, but he stopped me.
He asked for my number and I happily provided it

As my friends and I returned home,
We all gossiped about our misadventures
My excitement and interest was peaking
As I waited for his first message

Off to the Races
The two of us began to meet at his place
He didn't have a car,
But I didn't mind the drive across town
We saw each other once or twice a week.
A first kiss is shared
Clothes fell away and we explored each other's bodies
His tight arms and firm torso felt nice as my tongue roamed south

We rolled together in bed,
Taking turns giving pleasure to one another
Light sighs and excited groans
Whispered like ancient secrets
We were careful and quiet
His mother is only a room away.

The night ventures past midnight
Such a shame that this holy sight,
Two gorgeous Black bodies
Praising the beauty of one another
was witnessed solely by the moon.
Her light cascaded through the window,
Casting long shadows throughout the room
Finally our dance of flesh and pleasure ended
We both sank into his bed

As we lay next to one another,
Arms wrapped around each other,
We'd talk for hours and watch trash TV.

Over the next month, we would have many late night rendezvous
We talk about the mysteries of life and I find that he's a witch too
I am happy to share my knowledge on the subject
He was so eager to learn more

I brought him to different student-run clubs
Introduced him to my social groups
My friends accepted him in with ease
He was my boyfriend after all,

Boyfriend.
We made it official on my birthday.
A surprise I didn't reject
I enjoyed our time and clearly he did too

We had many talks
Including talks about my gender
I was finally beginning to socially transition
I made a simple request
Don't call me a guy
I wasn't a dude or a bro
And I was definitely not a man
Never use boyfriend,
I hated being introduced as a boyfriend
We both agreed we didn't like the use of partner
It sounded far too old and dated for an early 20 something

My pronouns are they/them
Refer to me as such and never use he/him
Getting misgendered always boiled my skin
I didn't want that from the person I was dating

These requests were thrown to the gutter
I actually don't remember if Jacob actually *ever* used the right ones
He, him, and his thrown casually around me
They all cut into my being with little effort

The first of many red flags, but I didn't address them at the time
Things were good between us for the most part
I enjoyed being around him
Loneliness was kept at bay when he was around

I was content.

Then the radio silence began....

His Next Trick: A Disappearing Act
Silence

That has always been a hard thing for me to deal with
I ask for communication
Jacob ignores me for days at a time without response
Excuse after excuse floods in before the silence dominates once again

"Where are you?"

My mind is clouded with darkness.
I reach out for him like I had done so many nights before,
But this time, there is no answer
I'm left scrambling on my own
Trying to stay afloat in a hurricane

I finally get to the eye of the storm and He finally answers.
I sigh and row my lifeboat to him
I arrive and expect warmth and kindness
Instead I am met with coldness and indifference
He gaslights me and makes the silence my fault
He is an expert dancer as he prances around responsibility

I'm tired and give him one more chance.
I plead that I need something, anything from him
He spits another lie in my face instead

Dumbfounded, utterly speechless
How could he be so cold?
We had spent many warm nights together
I couldn't believe this was it
After all we shared, this was how repaid me

I left and vowed to never return
I boarded my lifeboat once again
The hurricane is in full swing and I'm alone once more
This time is different though
Spite rises in my chest, anger hiss off my tongue,
I put my head down and row my heart out

I have plenty of fury to make it through to safety

I don't need a man who will lie to me
Make everything my fault
Disappear and reappear as he pleases
My feelings and thoughts be damned
I didn't need a emperor,
I needed a partner.

I can easily find another man to fill his spot
One who will treat me with respect
One who will respect my pronouns
One who will respect me and my needs
And in return I would give him the same respect

I've already seen this movie
Men have disrespected me in the past
I refuse to let it happen again

For the first time in a long while,
I took a stand for myself
It felt damn good to care about my own feelings

A month or two pass without him and I'm okay
I go on a few dates and meet some great people
I was at peace and having good experiences with kind strangers

It was all fun and games until the truth was finally revealed to me

Truth Comes to the Light
I meet someone online and we go on a few dates together
They know my most recent ex, Jacob.
A simple question was the last straw
To break open a mountain of deception
My new friend and I were both confused to learn
We were both dating him at the same time

Rewind back to Halloween,
They were inside while I flirted with Jacob at the front door
Jacob began to distance himself from my new friend
Prioritized me for a few months and then switched.
When they both started reigniting their relationship,
Jacob began to ignore me

A game of tug of war I wasn't aware of
He had found a way to get the best of both worlds
And no one spotted the deception right before our eyes
A true magician with a large bag of tricks and illusions

We both sat in the light of the truth
Anger flared in me once more
That bastard decided to pull me in through the back door of his home
My friend was the loving wife so what did that make me?
The Other Woman.
The one who came in on the weekend or late at night
But I could never stay for the sunrise

Hindsight illuminated so much in a matter of seconds
He never introduced me to anyone in his life
They would know the truth
Although we always attended my events,
I never got a glimpse into his world
I was always separated by a thin veil that I couldn't see
How did I not even notice?

The story makes so much sense,
But I could never see that plot twist coming
Betrayed is only the beginning of the avalanche of emotions

He wanted his cake and to eat it too
To this day, Jacob has the audacity
to pretend like nothing is wrong with what he did
I suppose I will never understand him

A simply reality that I must let go and move forward
It's the only way to keep moving forward,
I can't afford to look back at this train wreck

In the Dark Part 2
Being alone isn't always terrible
I have learned that I can take myself out and treat myself.
I go to the movies and live musical productions alone
That time is sacred for me, though

"I don't need someone to intrude"
That's what I repeat to myself
This mantra only works for a short duration

Then Life chips away at my way of thinking
I see couples holding hands in the street
An open declaration of their love
Such a beautiful sight,
But I try not to notice because I already know the consequence
Soft smiles and little laughter with one another as they step in unison
They whisper secrets of the universe to one another
Together

Water wells in my eyes
As the absence of warmth comes into full focus
I am not like them and I'm starting to wonder
Will I ever be part of that world?

It hurts me more and more as time treks by
Each couple I encounter slash a new wound into my heart
I try to stand tall as I bleed from the inside out
I am happy for their commitment,
but there is still a sting that burns into my nature

Where is my 'happily ever after'?
Has my Prince Charming in shining armor run into trouble?
I'm afraid that he may have saved the wrong girl
Now who will be here for me when I fall from the heavens?

Why does everyone else get to have their fairy tale ending?
Their life is presented in 4K High Definition
I live in a dull black and white cinema.
Grays invade once in a while to spice up my existence

That's my reality
My final chapter in my book…
What a tragic defeat,
A sad end to a truly sad tale.

Fighting Off the Gray
I must stay distracted.
That's how you outrun that pest named loneliness
I run as fast as my legs can carry me
The dark clouds paints over my life
Even the greatest moments live in grayscale,
Yet I still try my old tricks in hopes of a different outcome

Life starts to get a little more color
As I retreat to the closest gay bar
Men, scores and scores of men, fill my sight
I accept empty promises from these lustful men
Their eyes tell all their secrets
As their mouths smooth talks my zipper down

Pleasure can be a fun getaway adventure
Color splashes all around me.
Sadly it never lasts long
Once the climax hits,
The gray begins to return to the edges of my world

What's next? Alcohol
Self-medication brings a funky rose tint that I can tolerate.
A dull smile spread across my lips
The pain from all the universe numbs
And for a brief moment of reprieve,
I don't feel the ache that plagues me everyday
The dark clouds are holding and they don't venture closer

Loneliness loosens its grip around my throat
It leaves me for an hour or two
It knows I can't stay drunk forever

The dark clouds are a model for patience
They lurk in the distance
Looking for the most unexpected chance to pounce upon their prey
I dance for hours as the world spins off-center

For a moment, I exist in a world...
A world that isn't ruled by racing thoughts
For just a small moment,
I exist in a world that doesn't feel oppressive
I jot down a mental note

Peace is possible

Happiness by myself can be achieved
Held as the standard baseline
I can be satisfied,
Really and truly satisfied
I'll get there one day.

Hope holds my hand as the dark clouds advance once more
The rose color turns gray once again
I lower my head in defeat

Welcome back, old friend.
You never stay away for long, do you?

In the Dark - Part 3
I have wonderful friends who mean the world to me,
They have been by my side since the beginning of college
They welcomed me with open arms and open hearts
They hold my hand and love me harder than most folks

So why do I feel so alone in a room full of people?
This isn't like before where none of the people care
Every single one of my friends here love me
I can feel their warmth and it's genuine

When will I accept the love they placed at my altar?
When will loneliness leave me?
Even in the happiest moments of my life,
I feel a little sadness on the edge of my reality

Why can't I just accept that people care about me and believe in me?
Why can't I just be happy with the way my life is?
How can I expect to go on when my brain wants to self-destruct?

Even in the good times of my life,
Self-sabotage could wreck everything at any moment
I can't afford to play chicken with a real point of no return
I look into a mirror and stare straight into my own eyes

"When will you finally accept that you are
worthy of receiving genuine love and affection?
You are more than the lies that plays on repeat inside your mind
You are a good person…
I AM a good person!"

A Hope Meditation

This too shall pass
The Sun will rise again
Everyone forgets the warmth of the daylight
when they're standing in the darkness of Night.

She will rise again
Just like me
I too shall rise
It's only a matter of time

Chapter 4
Finding Balance

Change of Season - Part 2

As the sun sets in the autumn sky,
Golden light cascades across the landscape

Yellow leaves in the neighborhood
Catch in the crisp fall breeze.
They flutter in a dance of beauty and grace.
Orange leaves cling to their branches.
They whisper a song of farewell
As the season hurries past them
Brown leaves, tattered and dry,
Coat the ground for as far as the eye can see.
They are brittle and tired
The sudden temperature shift is a shock to the system

Nature, raw and beautiful, prepares for the next step
Something in the air is soft and comforting
I am preparing for my own next step
Five long years of undergraduate education comes to a close.
In this last year of my journey, Franklin stepped into my life
As I was ending one chapter, we were just beginning a new one.

I walk by his side down the street,
We gaze in awe as we continue
Through the wonderland of orange and yellow and brown
Hands clasped tightly to one another
As if they are afraid of missing a tender moment

Laughter is carried on the wind
Happiness is in full bloom between us
While the rest of the world shrinks away from the building cold,
We stand together
Keeping each other warm with our presence alone

Even with the bitter wind howling protest,
We are still strong and steady
Our love is capable of weathering any storm that'll come our way
Finally, peace doesn't feel like a distant fantasy anymore
It's my reality

Desire
Our bodies blend into one another
Your end is just the beginning for me
Hands gliding down soft skin
I yearn for your gentle touch
I crave your ridges and valleys
I want to explore every inch of you
I'm in pure bliss as you lay on me,
Feeling every kiss with a sense of urgency
I want you, every last drop of you
Swallow you whole so we can become one
Finding everlasting peace
Finding a never ending paradise
Finding the love I was destined to have…

Living in Color
Looking into your eyes,
I see a colorful galaxy swirl within you
It is beautiful and vast and magical
I can look into your eyes and never tire of the sight

My hand travels down your body
This heat meeting my touch feels foreign
You don't feel cold like the other men I've been with
I finally feel safe and warm in this bed with you

I get lost in the swirl of your hair
It showers me in rainbows and awe
Our lips dance a beautiful tango
As we forget the world around us

All I need, all I want, is for you to be by my side forever
The world is more vibrant when you're next to me
It's you and me against the world,
And I feel good about these odds
They won't know what hit 'em!

Polyamory
I have heard this term before but didn't know what it meant
Of course I knew the definition,
It was a hot topic in the media.
I just didn't grasp what that meant until I met Franklin.
It was the first time I ever been in a polyamorous relationship

We had to learn how to communicate our needs,
Especially since there were three people in the mix
And we all didn't date each other

Polyamory taught me how to set boundaries
I enforced my own as well as navigating others
It taught me love didn't have to be segregated

My love didn't have to be reserved for one person
It shaped my friendships in ways I never imagined possible
My love deepened for my friends, family, and partner.

Why should I pour all my energy into one person?
Someone who could leave at any moment?
Instead I can invest more into my friends who definitely deserve it
While simultaneously cultivating it with someone new in my life
A new person who brings a special meaning and connection

Some people have an abundance of love to show the world
They will care for complete strangers as if they are long-lost family
There's so much hate and judgement in the world
Why does love have to limit itself to a one spouse?

Eclipse
What do you do when you can't make the world shine
For the one who's brighter than the sun?

They mean the world to me
I want to protect them from harm,
But they have that same darkness I once had

Depression and anxiety reign king and queen
I want to overthrow the monarchy,
But I am simply one person

I hold onto my love as they float through the stars
I wait patiently on the ground as they crash back into orbit
I hate to see them fall
I feel so helpless
Spinning, tossing, turning,

Life hits me in the stomach
I watch them fight their own demons
I want to rescue them
I want to save them

I want to love them so hard that all the demons run for the hills
Running with their tails between their legs
But I can't do that
And that hurts even more than the loneliness I faced

I wish with all my heart that I could have been enough
But unfortunately I am only human
Heroes live in comic books
Gods hide in myths and tales
We humans must sit in the darkness of the valley

I see him, alone in the darkness,
I do the only thing I can do
I sit next to them and hold them tight
"Everything will be okay", I say as I kiss their forehead
I don't really know if it's true,

But I know that's what I need when I get in this headspace

I will sit with you for as long as you will let me
You don't have to fight alone,
You have me now,
You always will.

The Final Straw
Days and Days and Days
That's how it happens
Days of darkness morph into weeks
Weeks transforms into months

I begin to wonder if we will ever get back to the space before
Their boat is rowing farther and farther away
The seas churns into a choppy, rough mess
The lifeboat struggles to stay afloat
I call their name but only my echo replies

There are moments where they come back to me
Lucid and whole and real like before
We embrace and hold one another as hard as we can

"I don't want to lose you"

As quick as they come, they leave once again
Their departure hurts too much

The silence has always sliced away from my sanity
This time it feels like the knife is all the way to the hilt
The blade twists clockwise,
Ripping me open
Deeper and deeper

I wish to scream out in pain, but I don't
No one would be there to respond anyway

When Love Reaches Its Limit - Part 2

How do you get the strength to hurt someone you love?
How do you find the courage to leave
when things finally come to a close?

Another saga reaches a point of no return
I see the writings on the wall
But I close my eyes as hard as I can
Maybe things will change enough to be close to normal
Something that is similar to what was before…

I know humans can't recreate the past
If you try, it will only cause pain and suffering
You look into the eyes of the truth and feel true heartbreak

Will I submit to what is right?
Or will I cling to a worse lie?
Yearning for change can motivate us to do crazy acts of passion
Acts that harm,
Acts that damage beyond repair,
Acts that you can't take back…

I stand at a crossroad
I don't dare to move
What is the right choice and which is the wrong one?
Only time will reveal the answer,
But do I have that luxury right now?

Goodbye Love

I just came to say Goodbye, Love
I can't wait around any longer
I don't know what to say anymore
I'm afraid if I say anything,
I'll retreat back to the safety of darkness
I can't tell which hurts more.
The insufferable silence
Or leaving someone I love so much
I think I might always love them,
No matter what...

I wish things were different
I wish you lived closer
Ever since you left Grand Rapids,
The distance became longer than just a few hundred miles

I wish we could go back to the beginning
Back when magic was alive and well
When I could see the galaxy in your eyes,
Now I don't see anything and that terrifies me

I wish for a million things,
But what I wish the most is for you to finally be happy and free
You are so smart and talented and kind,
The darkness wouldn't show you that and I can't do it alone
I don't have that much strength

I pray that one day you will knock on my door…
You will always be greeted with a hug
Whenever our paths cross again,
I will still be in love with you.
I don't think I will ever stop loving you
I'm so sorry

I guess without further ado
Goodbye, My Dearest Love
Until we meet again.
Sincerely, Artemis

A Game of Desire
Chatter fills the dimly-lit room
Raised voices all fight for attention
The alcohol-soaked bar-top glisten from the TV light
Pop music videos play on the screen as speakers blare

You sit across from me
A sly smile pulls me in
Your hand slides to my inner thigh
I return your smile and giggle a little

We talk back and forth
It feels like we are playing tennis
You sure are a smooth talker
I can't get enough of your silky words
Your wit and banter keep me on my toes,
But I know how to surprise you too.

You move, then I counter
I advance, and you defend
A sweet tango fueled by liquor and lust
A dangerous combination for a summer night
Desire lingers around us as we wage our battle

Who will be the first to get what they want?
What do you want?
And more importantly,
What do I want?

Empty Gestures in Empty Bedrooms - Part 2

Laying there next to you,
I felt a vast nothingness swallow me whole

You slept soundly, softly
I swung in chaos, despair
The whole world flooded into my mind

No one can handle the secrets of the universe alone
No one should go through the Valley of Despair alone,
But I had to...
I ventured because you left me to the dogs!
To fight the darkness alone

That really hurt me
I helped you face the demons last time
Hours of comfort and attention
In the middle of the night in a strange setting
The park was cold and the wind blew through me
I felt a chill I could never escape

It's strange how this bed feels colder than that night
On the park bench at 3 in the morning
I can't even get a fucking embrace from you!
A limp hand reach out to me from a turned back
Is this sleepy, half-assed gesture supposed to comfort me?
News flash, it doesn't.
It hurt me even more

I can't believe my anger in this moment
My sadness
I'm not okay

But I will be one day
I have to,
Simply for my own sanity

I can do better than this
I deserve more than this cold bedroom and these empty gestures...

Cotton Candy
Light, Fluffy, Sweet
The flavor sticks to my tongue
Swirling and spinning

The universe dance in his iris
I can see so much in them
Wonder, desire, affection, trust, hope

Our lips meet and fireworks erupt between our bodies
The orbit of our bodies pull each other closer
Curiosity peaks as our hands begin to travel south
Garments fly and scatter across his room

Light sighs of pleasure erupt as the warmth of his mouth
Touches and licks and kisses my bare skin
He adventures across my valleys and plains
Ecstasy and lust combine as I return the favor
He gives, then I give, and so on and so forth
A tug of war of passion and pleasure

He pauses, an idea comes to his brilliant mind
He grabs some cotton candy and take a bite
A bit hangs from his lips as he return to me
I nibble off the bit and our lips meet in the middle

The sugar and pleasure mix well
He grabs more cotton candy
He places the pieces around my body
One by one, he begins to lick every piece from my body

I can see the delight in his eyes
I bet he can see the desire in mine too
I smile in a way I haven't in months

We play back and forth for hours
Two souls having a wonderful time in the secret of his bed
I can't stop smiling
This was the sweetest experience I've had in a very long time

Aiming for a Better Version
I want to have sex with people who adore me
People who have lust pouring from their very being
Those who are aware of my wit and charm
The ones who think my body is beautiful

I can get sex, that has never been an issue,
My issue is getting sex from people who want me
Not trying to simply get off for themselves

I want someone to explore my body
As I navigate their hills and valleys,
I want them to do the same to me
Make me feel seen
Make me feel things I have never felt before
Connect on a level that can never be truly explained

Someone who puts me first, above all others.
I'm not a consolation prize.
I'm not the runner up who gets sloppy seconds
I want to be the sun in their universe
Maybe then I won't feel so small

I want to have sex with someone who loves me
Maybe I'll find that person one day
There's over 6 billion people
One has to be for me? Right?

Chapter 5
A New Dawn

This chapter is dedicated to all the people who love me
Your support has been monumental and this is a small thank you
I couldn't acknowledge everyone here,
But there's always more books to write.
This won't be my last book, I promise.

Love Redefined
College was a very important time for me
I experienced a lot and grew into the person I am today
I learned a lot of skills that comes in handy in my career path
I also learned a lot about myself from those I surrounded myself with

My family came together in order to survive
We all lived in a hectic and hostile environment
We leaned on one another for support
Different backgrounds can bring different skill sets
Various mindsets that taught me so much

They taught me how to be gentle with myself
They taught me that familial love isn't just reserved for blood relatives
They taught me how to be confident in my body

And most importantly,
They showed me how to be unapologetic about my existence
I didn't have to shrink myself in order to make others happy
I just have to be who I dream to be
These lessons and so many more stay with me each day

As a Black Queer person,
I find myself limited on which side I can showcase
In Black spaces, my queerness was shoved into the back
In Queer spaces, my Blackness was seen as either a threat
Or a chase for sexual satisfaction through racist exoticism

Here with my QTPOC family, I didn't have to limit myself
I could be myself and not worry about what people thought
They just loved me and accepted me as their own
I found unconditional love in their arms

They saved my life countless times and continue to save me
As darkness falls and the future is even bigger and scarier,
I know I will make it because I have my chosen family by my side

They have all shown me how love can actually be
Both my relationships and my perspective

Has been radicalized and revolutionized
The core group of us has always pushed me
To be the best version of myself I could achieve
I shouldn't have to limit myself
Life offers so many possibilities

Everyone has brought a special purpose into my life
A lesson that has guided me through some dark times
They continue to be my light to this very day
I truly love them all with all my heart

Ode to the Strongest Woman I Know, My Mother
I can't write a book about love without mentioning you, Mama
After all, you showed me how to love and care for others
I may have learned a lot while I was two and a half hours away,
But the lessons you gave me will never leave me,
No matter how far away I travel

My mom showed me how to treat others simply by her actions
You taught me to treat every stranger with respect and dignity
And most important of all,
You taught me that kindness is the easiest way to greet a stranger

"You have no idea what type of day a person is having,
But if you're nice and show them a good time,
You might be able to get them to smile and laugh a little bit.
And that could be the highlight of their day, you never know.
At least they forgot about their troubles for a moment.
You never know the impact you can have on someone."
You told me that when I was 18,
But you showed me that through your actions years before.

My mom is the sweetest person I know
She would do anything for her family
She has done countless services for my family
Her warmth and kindness is felt by everyone who meets her
She has been my rock for all of my life

Sometimes I hide the darkest moments from her
And that's because I don't want her to see that yet
I can't handle the thought of my mom seeing me in my darkness
I know she won't judge me,
But I simply don't want to cause her anymore pain
Life is hard and I don't want to make it any harder for her

My mother, though a saint, doesn't always get it right,
But she always does her best to learn how to be better
That's what truly matter at the end of the day

My mother goes to work every day
She takes care of business at home
She carries the weight of so many and always have her head up
I wish I could be as strong as her one day

My mother works herself to the bone in order for me to be where I am
She sacrificed so much and has never asked for anything in return
Now in my adulthood with much reflection on the past,
I finally am able to piece together only a fraction
Of what she has done for me over the years

I will never be able to repay her for all the things she has done

She is my true definition of love
She is my true definition of strength
She is the entire universe
Placed simply and elegantly into a human vessel

I love you so much Mama
I hope I can make you proud one day

Love Letter for CD
Music videos play on the Smart TV
We try to suppress our gasps and awe because it's 3 in the morning
Yet we are still up with one another
These long nights can make anyone forget the outside world exists
In hard times like these, I really need that

Distraction after distraction carry our attention
YouTube rabbit holes,
Re-watching The Walking Dead,
Netflix Original Series and documentary binges,
Story ideas and the outlines we said but never wrote down
You really helped me through a rough year

Your encouragement really does help me want more for myself
I may feel stuck sometimes but you show me that anything is possible
Your love is supportive and creative
But you aren't afraid to also hold me accountable
My ideas can be quite lofty and you help me think out logistics
Sometimes I need to be brought back down to earth
That's the only way something tangible can occur

Life is a whirlwind for me in my mind,
But the spinning doesn't feel as bad when you're around
No amount of words can express how much I appreciate you
You've done a lot for me and I can never thank you enough
I may have tried with this poem
But I can't describe all the feelings I still have

You are so smart, talented, creative, and a wonderful human
I'm proud of you for carving a path for yourself
You are being creative and getting paid now,
But you still aim for something much larger.
You will reach it one day
I can't wait to see your vision become reality
It will be beautiful and caring and thoughtful, just like you.
I'm lucky to call you my friend

Love Letter for JD
Long car rides with the music blasting
Tasty food fill our table while a movie drone on in the background
Late nights we would spend talking with all of our friends
Or listening to a No Sleep Podcast if we are feeling spooky enough
Horror movies was our specialty that not everyone could handle,
But we would watch marathons of old and new, good and cheesy
We would never tire of our binges

We spent a lot of free time watching shows together and
Talking shit about whatever foolishness we witness
I remember us laughing so hard we can barely breathe
How are we still alive after so many laughing fits?
Only God knows I suppose

Who knew the quiet guy who had amazing nails
In one of my Greek myth class back in freshman year of college
Would become one of my best friends and we'd live together?
Created a bond that I would consider family
We shared our living space with so many people
Opened our home to so many who needed refuge
A safe place to rest their heads and fill their stomachs
They could find a home with us while they figured their situation out

You are so kind and loving and understanding
You hold your head high and speak clearly for all to hear
Your opinion matters and you know it
That's a powerful statement in a society
That wants to silence Black Queers like us.

Your love shows me that there is still hope for a better tomorrow
I know I'm not the best roommate to have,
But I want to thank you for all you do here
And for putting up with me for so long
I don't know if I could even do something like that.
I know you are going to achieve massive tasks with your brilliant mind
The world is gonna change because of you
I can't wait to witness what your future holds
It will be as bright and beautiful as you are

Love Letter for DH
Walking into the Center and seeing a Black Queer person working
That was monumental for a young queer in the making.
Getting to know you was even more spectacular and magical
Fashion and style were your domain
No one could ever dream of dressing like you
Pop culture, current events in general, was your jam
You know what's going on 9 times out of 10
Your opinion poised neatly with the information given
Our fucked up society could never silence you.
You are so well spoken and hold nuanced opinions.
Your perspective makes others think critically.
Even though you know so much information
And have so many cool ideas,
You can break down the theories
In ways people can truly understand and swallow.
Accessibility is a staple of your praxis

You not only carved space out for everyone to feel comfortable in,
You also cared for a marginalized subgroup within a marginalized group
You lead the way for future generations to follow so they too can thrive
Such a light and beautiful spirit shines from within you

We laughed, we sang and danced, we marched, we cried,
We supported one another through a lot
I have witnessed you grow and expand yourself and those around you
It's a wonderful energy to experience
I'm so lucky you graced me with your presence

You inspired me to spread my own wings and explore myself
You gave me the permission I needed to be better
You showed me that I was worthy of love
I can never thank you enough for that

D, you mean the world to me
I'm so lucky to have you as part of my family
You helped me in ways I could never describe
Even with all the words in the English language.
I love and appreciate you

Love Letter for EE
Your poetry was meaningful, beautiful, raw, and genuine
I was encapsulated the second you opened your mouth at open mic night
You have always been a divine storyteller
Your Imagination soars miles above all the rest on Earth
Poets usually talk of superficial things that amount to little
You never had to do that
Your poems spoke of real emotions, complex feelings
That's the first time I knew you were special and unique and wonderful

The next time we crossed was at a Stage after party
It was after the first show I ever performed in
We sat together in that stairway and gossiped
Mostly about the straight antics around us
A lifeboat in the sea of heteronormativity
Alcohol fueled me to talk to you, the gods know how terrified I was
A normal person couldn't casually walk up to divinity, Heavens NO!
But you were secretly a lot more down to earth than I anticipation
A cool person who I could be friends with

We shared more and more moments as time marched on
Conferences, parties, potlucks, late night gatherings,
Shared birthday celebrations,
We did it all and grew so much closer than I could ever imagine
We discuss secrets of the universes under the light of the moon
Secrets of the past that still haunts us like a ghost in a haunted house
Plans of the future and hopes for what life could hold
Nerd out around our mutual love for D&D and fantasy themed worlds
Our fire burned the city anew and no one could stop us
Living with you has been a blessing
I appreciate every moment we share
Life can be hard and overwhelming,
But I know we can make it through together
You have so much compassion and kindness
And a drive that nothing can impede
I know you're going to be a great nurse that will change the game
Set an example of how to care for others
While giving them dignity and respect they deserve
You're going to be Amazing

Love Letter for FM
You have always been a big fiery ball of energy
You rushed into the Center one day and instantly ran into my heart
The pure, radiant energy you gave could illuminate a whole city
Happiness and love filled the room when you were there
Then life tried to swallow us in helplessness and despair
Depression, anxiety, a house that was made of cards and bedbugs,
It was a rough time,
But you always supported me through it and
I tried my best to do the same for you
Your intentions were honest and meaningful
I never had to guess where you were
We talked freely and bluntly, no fluff or bullshit was between us
I loved that about us, I still do honestly

As time shifted, we stayed connected the best we could
Then the pandemic started and I felt more alone than ever
We soon found a new way to interact that was social-distance friendly
Video Games, from our respective homes
Though I sat alone in the living room,
It felt like you were next to me as we fought our way to victory royale
You always asked "how's Artemis today?"
That was needed much more than you know
It helped me conceptualized the feelings of the day

I watched you grow so much in the last few years
We have supported and loved one another
You shown me what love can be
Sweet, funny, chaotic,
Ready to defend your friend's honor at any moment's notice
I want to thank you for being my friend
I can't wait to see all the awesome things you'll do
I know you can achieve so many wonderful things
Grad school is only the tip of the iceberg for you

You're a fighter
A defender for transgender and queer kids
The idiots in the world better shape up or else they will feel your fire
The World will know your name one day…

Love Letter to AS & CS
I met you both at a LGBT event downtown
Music blasted and people danced like tomorrow would never come
I have met a lot of people during my time in Grand Rapids,
But I could never imagine what came next
AS invited me over for a game night
CS was an excellent host and welcomed me into their home
They both showed me what love could look like

A family with many parts and pieces
That joined together to create a beautiful collage.
The first time I ever saw a successful polyamorous love
The first time I saw parenting in a new light
A wonderful child who amazes me every time I see her
She's being raised by a true, loving village
Real adults with real results of a future
Only seen in the IMAX of human imagination
A new potential turned flesh and breathing right before my very eyes

Those nights drinking weren't superficial like others I had in college
These nights were warm and sweet as hot cocoa on a winter day
Philosopher would be happy to join the conversations we had
You both gave me the power to dream of a queer-er future for myself
You gave me the space to create the adult that I wanted to be

Not only that,
I feel like you listened to my opinion and wanted to hear my thoughts
In a life where silence ruled, you pulled me to the front and said
My thoughts mattered and you wanted to hear them
A complete stranger at one point,
Yet you welcomed me in like an old friend
There is so much love between not just the two of you,
But everyone who walks into your home
It's a healing sensation that I can never fully describe

I appreciate you both so much
I can't wait for us to make more memories once things are safe again
I love you and your family so much
I wish nothing but the best and happiness for you all

Love Letter to E&K
When I think of you,
I think of many things that can be equated to the both of you
A love that can overcome any obstacle
Food and joy and all sorts of debauchery deep into the night
Makeup and dressing up for drag performances
A hazy car as we travel to Cedar Point for Gay Days
The summer sun setting on the horizon
Hiking through the mountains of Southern California

Staying with you for weeks on end and you both never got tired of me
Never made me feel unwelcome
We have so many fond memories and I care about you both so deeply
Your happiness makes me happy
I hope to find a love that is as nice, caring, and understanding as yours
It is clear there is a true connection between your souls
A level of complexity that no one can possibly fathom

Your wedding day still plays in my mind sometimes
The glances you both share communicate so much
A matter of seconds passed and yet you both said a million things
That day was simply pure and magnificent and beautiful

We may stay on different sides of the country now,
But I will always love you both so much
Maybe one day I will finally move out West like you've asked me to do
You've asked at least a hundred times already,
But you know how stubborn I can be.

Regardless, we will see each other soon enough
We will begin again as if no time has passed at all
I can't wait to see the future you both create

Kindness Within
I wake up and I feel different
Tiredness still fills my eyes and clouds my mind
I fight my way out of bed and into the bathroom
I look in the mirror and I smile
I used to struggle with this,
Seeing my body always had negative feedback,
But not today
My mind is a little nicer to myself

"It's okay. Where you are is okay.
That is enough and change will come when it needs to.
I am brave. I am strong. I am enough."

On this journey to find love,
I think I might have actually found it
Just not in the way I imagined.
It's not like in the romance movies
The bland, straight, whitewashed bull crap isn't meant for me anyway
This love is understanding, kind, firm, and unyielding
I will admit, some days are darker than others,
But at least I'm still here, trying my best
I never imagined I would reach this far
Death lurked about for years
I always assumed I would never make it past 21

I think I was fed a lot of information about what love is supposed to be
It took a lot of unlearning and rebuilding on my own
There was pleasure, pain, happiness, sorrow, and so much more
My journey was hard and it isn't over yet

I met people who tried to burn me down,
Take away all that was sacred and meaningful to me.
I met people who built me up like a cathedral,
Delicate details and beautiful archways that can hold space for others.
I don't regret any step I took in this journey
All my past decisions and company I kept has shaped me into who I am

I had to experience something so radical and rigorous

In order for me to finally get the power I needed to fly
I'm done falling and spiraling into darkness
My family and friends provide the wind I have been missing all along
I wasn't meant to do this alone

Air rush pass my face and the sun shines on my skin
This feeling of peace is even better than I imagined
My eyes have opened to the realm of possibilities in front of me
I wish I could fly forever and never return to Earth,
But I must land and recover once in a while
No one can fly forever, we all must rest eventually.
And I'm lucky to have special people stand beside me
Even when the storm clouds come in
And the thunder crashes and lightning flashes,
I know I can weather anything with the ones who I love
We can help each other through the darkness

A realization washes over me
I smile wider than ever before
I'm not alone anymore.
I have people who will fight for me
Love me hard and laugh even harder
I'm not as worried about the future anymore
Of course I still fear what tomorrow holds,
I have depression with a sprinkle of anxiety,
I will always worry about things outside of my control
But I am forcing my mind to face reality
I love others and I am loved in return

So we have finally reached the end of this book
It's been a journey with ups and downs
And it still isn't over just yet
I just have one last request
One last question that will never have a true answer
It always shifts and changes with time and experience,
But I will try and answer in this moment
If I need to adapt it later, I won't sweat it.
Some things in life are ever-changing.
I have to ask myself, what is love?

What Love Actually Is

Love is more than just one person trying to morph themselves into something that loses all meaning and authenticity in order to become an "other half"

Love is the feeling of warm hands holding yours in the dead of night
Telling you "Everything will be okay" and you believe them.

Love is your family coming together
Scraping up all we have so everyone can eat.

Love is accepting someone for their flaws and all
And pushing them to see a better destiny for themselves.

Love is doing whatever you can to help out when you have
The time and energy and resources to assist others.

Love is creating a space where anyone can spread their wings
And fly to a future they dream and crave.

Love is allowing distance when times get too rough,
But you leave the door open for their return.
(Whenever that may be
Because sometimes people don't come right back
Everyone has their own journeys to take, and that's okay)

Love is all the possibilities you dream turning into reality
Anything is possible once you have the strength to not only imagine it
You also have to work towards it.

Love is sharing a blanket on a beach as the sun sets across a Great Lake
Sitting with the one person you want to spend the rest of your days with.

It's all these things and so much more
And it isn't meant just for one person
Love is for friends, family, lovers, and yourself too
You don't have to reserve it only for other people,
You can turn it inward as well
That's how you thrive instead of just simply surviving.

Love can help you overcome so many obstacles,
And that's because Love brings Hope
Hope for a better tomorrow,
Even when the darkest night drift into days and weeks
Hope can pull you back from the brink of death and destruction

You don't have to reserve hope for only other people
You deserve it just as much as everyone else
I deserve the world and so do you
It's not a competition to see who's on top
That's a capitalistic scam fed to us by Uncle Sam

Love,
Real love is collectively rising above the odds
We can all make it up to the top of the mountain
There's enough to go around for everyone
So if I reach a summit first,
I will go back for the ones I love and help them up
I will proudly reach out my hand to hoist them up,
Because I know they would do the same for me too

I pray everyone can find a family like mine
A family that holds one another in times of need,
Celebrates the victories whenever they come
A victory for one of us is a victory for all of us,
We laugh and live and cheer each other,
And most importantly,
We all try our best to be understanding and accepting of one another

We know we are all capable of doing marvelous things
Everyone has the power to shape their realities
We deserve peace and happiness and we will obtain that
We will fight side by side until that goal is reached

Standing together,
Until the Very End.

Made in the USA
Monee, IL
19 June 2021